Anonymous

# An Enquiry Into the Lawfulness and Expediency of Singing in Christian Worship

Anonymous

**An Enquiry Into the Lawfulness and Expediency of Singing in Christian Worship**

ISBN/EAN: 9783337034818

Printed in Europe, USA, Canada, Australia, Japan

Cover: Foto ©Lupo / pixelio.de

More available books at **www.hansebooks.com**

# AN ENQUIRY

INTO

## THE LAWFULNESS AND EXPEDIENCY

OF

# SINGING

# IN CHRISTIAN WORSHIP.

BY A

## Member of the Society of Friends.

*"Audi alteram partem."*

DARLINGTON :

HARRISON PENNEY, PRINTER AND STATIONER, PREBEND ROW.

LONDON : SAMUEL HARRIS AND CO., BISHOPSGATE ST.

1883.

Well, when I had thus put my ends together,
I shewed them others, that I might see whether
They would condemn them or them justify:
And some said, "Let them live;" some, "Let them die;"
Some said, "John, print it;" others said, "Not so;"
Some said, "It might do good;" others said, "No."
Now was I in a strait, and did not see
Which was the best thing to be done by me.
At last I thought, "Since you are thus divided,
I print it will;" and so the case decided.
"For," thought I, "some, I see, would have it done,
Though others in that channel do not run."
To prove, then, who advised for the best,
Thus I thought fit to put it to the test.

JOHN BUNYAN.

# AN ENQUIRY INTO THE LAWFULNESS AND EXPEDIENCY OF SINGING IN CHRISTIAN WORSHIP.

---

## IS SINGING LAWFUL?

### I.—BIBLE TESTIMONY.

"Preoccupation of the mind by fixed opinions leads to a wrong reading of any evidence. We unconsciously distort facts, or invent them, to support our favourite theories, and see everything through their medium. * * * Our conclusions are determined largely by our predispositions, and our prejudices, or prejudgments, in great measure monopolize our faculties. We are not so much ignorant as perverted. We see truth through a prism. We are so entirely the creatures of education, of the opinions of our neighbours and of our family, and of the thousand influences of life, that the only way we can hope to see truth in its own white and unbroken light is, as Christ tells us, by our becoming little children." [Geikie's "Life of Christ, 1879, vol. i. p. 108.]

In enquiring into the lawfulness of Singing in Christian worship, it is beside the question to cite the numerous advices and examples given in the Old

Testament as to this outward observance. The rites and ceremonies there enjoined were for Jews, but not always for Christians, "For the law having a shadow of good things to come, and not the very image of the things," "was our schoolmaster to bring us unto Christ, that we might be justified by faith. But after that faith is come, we are no longer under a schoolmaster." And further, as Christ came not to destroy but to fulfil the law, Himself declaring, "Till heaven and earth pass, one jot or one tittle shall in no wise pass from the law, till all be fulfilled," so it is equally useless to point to the practice of our Lord or His apostles previous to the resurrection, as examples, so far as regards Jewish rites and ceremonies, to be followed by Christians.

Heb. x. 1.

Gal. iii. 24, 25.

Matt. v. 18.

For a clear exposition and confirmation of Christian practice we must therefore confine ourselves to the inspired writings as contained in the Acts of the Apostles and the succeeding books of the New Testament.

Such passages then as the following are more or less relevant to our purpose.

Acts ii. 46, 47. [Of the believers] "And they, continuing daily with one accord in the Temple, and breaking bread from house to house, did eat their meat with gladness and singleness of heart, praising God, and having favour with all the people."

Acts iii. 8, 9. [Of the lame man healed.] "And he, leaping up, stood, and walked, and entered with them into the Temple, walking and leaping and praising God. And all the people saw him walking and praising God."

Acts xvi. 25. "And at midnight Paul and Silas prayed, and sang praises unto God : and the prisoners heard them."

Rom. xv. 9-11. "And that the Gentiles might glorify God for his mercy ; as

it is written, For this cause I will confess to thee among the
Gentiles, and sing unto thy name. And again he saith, Rejoice,
ye Gentiles, with his people. And again, Praise the Lord, all
ye Gentiles; and laud him, all ye people."

"For if I pray in an unknown tongue, my spirit prayeth, but _1 Cor. xiv. 14, 15._
my understanding is unfruitful. What is it then? I will pray
with the spirit, and I will pray with the understanding also: I
will sing with the spirit, and I will sing with the understanding
also."

"Be filled with the Spirit; speaking to yourselves in psalms _Eph. v. 18, 19._
and hymns and spiritual songs, singing and making melody in
your heart to the Lord."

"Let the word of Christ dwell in you richly in all wisdom; _Col. iii. 16._
teaching and admonishing one another in psalms and hymns
and spiritual songs, singing with grace in your hearts to the
Lord."

"For both he that sanctifieth and they who are sanctified are _Heb. ii. 11, 12._
all of one; for which cause he is not ashamed to call them
brethren, saying, I will declare thy name unto my brethren, in
the midst of the church will I sing praise unto thee."

"By him therefore let us offer the sacrifice of praise to God _Heb. xiii. 15._
continually, that is, the fruit of our lips giving thanks to his
name."

"Is any merry? let him sing psalms." _James v. 13._

"And they sung a new song, saying, Thou art worthy to take _Rev. v. 9._
the book, and to open the seals thereof."

"And they sung as it were a new song before the throne." _Rev. xiv. 3._

"And they sing the song of Moses the servant of God, and _Rev. xv. 3._
the song of the Lamb."

Before proceeding to a more definite consideration _The Holy Scriptures are the only divinely authorized record of Christian doctrines._
of any of these texts, we may observe that, in order to
bring any argument to a satisfactory conclusion, it is
absolutely necessary to have a well-defined ground
upon which each process of reasoning may be based;

and for those to whom the following thoughts are addressed, my fellow-members of the Society of Friends, such a standpoint has been laid down with combined clearness, simplicity, and fulness in the following declaration of the Yearly Meeting, in an Epistle issued in 1836 :—

"Christian Doctrine, Practice, and Discipline," c. i. p. 15, 5th edition, 1871.

"It has ever been, and still is, the belief of the Society of Friends, that the Holy Scriptures of the Old and New Testament were given by inspiration of God ; that therefore the declarations contained in them rest on the authority of God Himself ; and there can be no appeal from them to any other authority whatsoever : that they are able to make us wise unto salvation through faith which is in Christ Jesus ; being the appointed means of making known to us the blessed truths of Christianity : that they are the only divinely authorised record of the doctrines which we are bound as Christians to believe, and of the moral principles which are to regulate our actions : that no doctrine which is not contained in them can be required of anyone to be believed as an article of faith : that whatsoever any man says or does which is contrary to the Scriptures, though under profession of the immediate guidance of the Spirit, must be reckoned and accounted a mere delusion."

Taking the above as a definition .authoritatively given of the basis of our religious belief, we unhesitatingly declare that it is impossible to find anything in those Scriptures of Truth which, directly or indirectly, teaches that there are no circumstances or conditions of men in which the Holy Spirit can call for the Singing of Hymns in the public worship of God. Such a doctrine is nowhere to be found in them, and, consequently, is not "required of anyone to be believed as an article of faith."

Having thus disposed of the negative, we pursue the enquiry further to know whether the opposite be correct, viz., that there *are* circumstances and conditions of men where the Holy Spirit will call for the Singing of Hymns in public worship.

For the present we will confine our attention to two of the texts we have quoted, which are important as giving firstly, example, and secondly, precept.

*Example.* —"And at midnight Paul and Silas prayed, and sang praises unto God: and the prisoners heard them." Acts xvi. 25.

*Precept.* "Let the word of Christ dwell in you richly in all wisdom; teaching and admonishing one another in psalms and hymns and spiritual songs, singing with grace in your hearts to the Lord." Col. iii. 16.

The former proves, at least, that the two prisoners at Philippi sang with an audible voice (for "the prisoners heard them"), in the ascription of praise to God, one of the very purposes for which we meet together in our places for worship; the latter gives a direct command to the Church at Colosse to teach and admonish one another with the singing of hymns, &c. The two together surely proving that there *may* be cases where such exercises are called for in that worship which is "in spirit and in truth," and, as a

necessary corollary, that man should not, by word or
action, individually or collectively, interpose his veto
upon the carrying out of the revealed will of God in
this respect.

*Obj.* 1.—An objection brought to the former of
these texts is, that it does not relate to a meeting for
worship, and therefore is no example for our meetings.

*Ans.*—We reply in the words of the printed Epistle,

"Christian Doc-
trine, Practice,
and Discipline,"
ch. ii. § 1. p. 32.

1855 : "May we ever bear in mind, that it is not the
mere outward gathering together, but the inward
gathering of our hearts unto the Lord, that makes a
true meeting for worship. And how consoling is the
remembrance that this worship is not dependent upon
numbers : where two or three are gathered in the
name of Christ, there is a church, and Christ, the
living Head, in the midst of them."

*Obj.* 2.—Others again remark that the singing at
Philippi was in a meeting entirely composed of con-
verted believers, and their objection refers only to
singing in mixed gatherings.

We shall refer to this subject again ; for the present,
granting the character of the meeting at Philippi, we
yet would ask—Is there any good reason to suppose
that the outward visible church at Colosse was less
miscellaneous in character and composition than
churches now-a-days?

*Obj.* 3.—With regard to the latter text the objection

has been made that the singing it commands should be in our hearts alone, and that audible singing is not meant.

*Ans.*—The text, however, does not contain a word about "Singing in the heart." It does say that we are to sing with "*grace*" in the heart, just as Paul in the same epistle writes, "Let your *speech* be alway with grace." The context indeed proves that the un- Col. iv. 6. spoken melody of the heart is not exclusively referred to, for the command is to *teach* and *admonish* one another (thereby necessitating vocal utterances) "in psalms and hymns and spiritual songs."

*Obj.* 4.—It has been urged that the command to the church at Colosse was not intended to be used as an argument in favour of the liberty to Christians in all future time to sing under the guidance of the Spirit, but that it may rather be classed in the same category with those "*necessary things*," to abstain "from things strangled and from blood," which were written to the Gentiles after the Conference held in Jerusalem, as recorded in Acts xv., that is, as a temporary command under special circumstances, or in deference to long-established prejudices.

*Ans.*—The letter from the Conference was not the exclusive production of the apostles as an unbiassed expression of their individual feeling and judgment, but quite otherwise ; and remains to us a teaching lesson of their deep humility, in that, though acknow- ledged as Christ-sent messengers, they were so filled with that spirit of love and forbearance which must ever actuate the true Christian as to agree in the compromise which was written. For it *was* a compromise. "There had been much disputing." Peter had expressed the gospel truth, as recorded in the 11th verse, and we are left in no doubt as to the sentiments of Paul, but yet they were willing to unite in the sentence of James, and allow two of the commands of Moses (in themselves perfectly harmless and non-essential, for they were contrary to no command and violated no principle) to go forth to the Gentile converts as necessary to be observed for the preservation of peace and harmony in the church : whilst the Jewish converts at the Conference, with a liberality which becomes more astonishing the more we examine into it, yielded not only their standpoint as given in ver. 1, but sacrificed the influences and teachings of a lifetime, and with one accord coincided in the selection of those two commands only, out of the 10,000 Rabbinical Rules, the more or less complete observance of which had been their life-long test of religiousness and of patriotism.

On the other hand the example and precept we have quoted are those of the apostles themselves, given unbiassed in favour of Singing ; and the teaching of the New Testament, by the declaration of such service being acceptable in heaven itself (see the texts we have quoted on p. 7), however symbolical the language may be, leads us to infer that such service is neither unacceptable on earth, nor intended, like the precepts of Moses, to pass away with the ceremonies of the Law.

Acts xv. 7.

Acts xv. 2 & cf. Rom. iii. 24.

See Geikie's "Life of Christ," vol. i. p. 252.

See p. 9.

## II.—"QUAKER" TESTIMONY.

But, notwithstanding the clearness of the testimony of Scripture which we have adduced on the subject, there are very many amongst us who have grown up with a belief that these Scripture texts can all be reasoned away as satisfactorily as those which are so frequently misquoted in favour of War, Oaths, Sacraments, &c.; and that the Society of Friends as a religious Body has always objected to outward audible singing as a part of public worship.

The writer having never learned to sing, and prejudiced against the practice, acknowledges this to have been the case with himself. He remembers with what pain and oppressive sense of exclusion and want of communion he used to sit in meetings where singing was introduced. And it was not until he found that some had been led to walk in newness of life through the instrumentality of hymn-singing that he began to question his former scruples and to search the Scriptures to discover the mind of Truth, with the result he has already given.

But now another search commenced. Love and veneration mingled in the heart of the writer towards those by-gone worthies in the early history of our Society who were raised up for a special and noble purpose, whose book of daily study was the Bible, who were "deep in divine knowledge" and "richly endued with heavenly wisdom." Could it be possible that George Fox, Robert Barclay, and the generations of Friends since their time, professing to seek and be guided by the Spirit of Truth, and willing to bring every doctrine to the test of Scripture, had yet propounded what now appeared to have no Scriptural authority and to militate even against obedience to the Divine Will!

Very carefully were passed in review the "Journal of George Fox," Robert Barclay's "Apology," "The Book of Christian Doctrine, Practice, and Discipline," and the whole of the "Epistles of the Yearly Meeting." And with what result! A deeper appreciation than ever of the heavenly wisdom of those who gave full credence to the promise, "If any of you lack wisdom, let him ask of God, that giveth to all men liberally and upbraideth not: and it shall be given him." Not a sentence could be taken *in its connection* to uphold the old prejudice against singing: not a word to show that the doctrines of the Society were at variance with the teachings of the Bible, or that Quakerism was other than " Primitive Christianity revived."

*Jas. i. 5.*

In the "Book of Christian Doctrine, Practice, and Discipline" there is an entire absence of direct reference to the question of singing: a most significant fact when we remember how universal is the practice amongst the religious bodies around us.

Turning next to Barclay's "Apology," we find the opening of the argument concerning Worship in Proposition xi. reads thus : "All true and acceptable worship to God is offered in the inward and immediate moving and drawing of His own Spirit, which is neither

"Barclay's Apology," Manchester, 1850, Prop. xi. p. 100.

limited to places, times, nor persons. For though we are to worship Him always, and continually to fear before Him, yet as to the outward signification thereof, in *prayers, praises*, or *preachings*, we ought not to do it in our own will, where and when we will; but where and when we are moved thereunto by the stirring and secret inspiration of the Spirit of God in our hearts; which God heareth and acceptath of, and is never wanting to move us thereunto, when need is; of which He Himself is the alone proper judge," &c.

True it is that many Friends object to what they conceive to be the teachings of Barclay's "Apology." Provided the objection they take be legitimate, the real difficulty may be in the expression of Robert Barclay's views, and not in the soundness of his theology—and clearer statements will be found in other writings of the apologist. Let it be borne in mind that Barclay was no novice in the art of disputation; and that the power of the logician chiefly lies in the use of words which convey clearly his exact meaning. But the finer distinctions in the definition of words frequently vary with time and place, and though the words of Barclay were clear and intelligible to a Scotch Presbyterian in the reign of Charles II., they are sometimes not so clear to a Quaker intelligence in the reign of Queen Victoria. Take, for instance, the word *"praises"* in the last quoted extract. There are those who suppose it meant the silent gratitude of the heart, but the people of Aberdeen in 1675 had no difficulty in apprehending his true meaning to be the singing of *psalms and hymns and spiritual songs*, not *silently*, but, as he himself says in the quotation, as one of the "OUTWARD SIGNIFICATIONS" of worship.

" Apology,"
Prop. xi. § 9,
p. 167.

In the same sense we read the word "PRAISE" in the 9th Section of that Proposition. "God is not wanting to move in his children to bring forth words of exhortation or prayer, when it is needful ; so that of the many gatherings and meetings of such as are convinced of the truth, there is scarce any in which God raiseth not up some or other to minister to his brethren ; and there are few meetings that are altogether silent. For when many are met together in this one life and name, it doth most naturally and frequently excite them to *pray* and *praise* God, and stir up one another by mutual *exhortation* and *instructions;* yet we judge it needful there be in the first place some time of *silence,* during which every one may be gathered inward to the word and gift of grace, from which he that ministereth may receive strength to bring forth what he ministereth ; and that they that hear may have a sense to discern betwixt the precious and the vile, and not to hurry into the exercise of these things so soon as the bell rings, as other Christians do."

The context of the above points out pretty clearly what is meant, as also does that of the language used in the answers to Objection 3 to the 17th Section of the same Proposition, where we read at the commencement, "Some or other are still moved either to *preach, pray,* or *praise,"* and at the close, " I shall add something more particularly of *preaching, praying,* and *singing."*

' Barclay's
Apology,"
Manchester,1850
pp. 179, 180.

As we have just seen, however, Barclay does not confine himself to the word *"praise"* or *"praises."*

In the 10th Section he writes, "Jesus Christ, the author of the Christian religion, prescribes no set form of worship to His children, under the more pure administration of the new covenant, save that He only tells them, That the worship now to be performed is spiritual, and in the Spirit.  And it is especially to be observed, that in the whole New Testament there is no order nor command given in this thing, but to follow the revelation of the Spirit, save only that general one of meeting together; a thing dearly owned and diligently practised by us, as shall here-after more appear.  True it is, mention is made of the duties of *praying, preaching,* and *singing;* but what order or method should be kept in so doing, or that presently they should be set about so soon as the saints are gathered, there is not one word to be found; yea, these duties, as shall afterwards be made appear, are always annexed to the assistance, leadings, and motions of God's Spirit."

" Apology,
Prop. xi. § 10,
pp. 169, 170.

Here we are plainly given to understand that Robert Barclay, as the spokesman of the Society of Friends, considers *Singing* to be a *"duty,"* just as much as *praying* and *preaching,* and under the very same con-ditions—that is, "annexed to the assistance, leadings, and motions of God's Spirit."

In Sections xviii. to xxv. inclusive, Barclay defines
and defends the doctrines of Friends regarding
*preaching* and *praying*, and opens the next Section

"Apology,"
Prop. xi. § 26,
p. 190.

(xxvi.) with these words:—"As to the *singing of
Psalms*, there will not be need of any long discourse :
for that the case is just the same as in the two former
of *preaching* and *prayer*.   We confess this to be a part
of God's worship, and very sweet and refreshing, when
it proceeds from a true sense of God's love in the
heart, and arises from the divine influence of the
Spirit, which leads souls to breathe forth either a
sweet harmony, or words suitable to the present condition ; whether they be words formerly used by the
saints, and recorded in Scripture, such as the Psalms
of David, or other words ; as were the hymns and songs
of Zacharias, Simeon, and the blessed Virgin Mary."

And again, further on in the same section he proceeds, "That singing then that pleaseth Him must
proceed from that which is pure in the heart (even
from the Word of Life therein), in and by which,
richly dwelling in us, spiritual songs and hymns are
returned to the Lord, according to that of the apostle,
Col. iii 16."

*Obj.*—But we have heard it urged as an objection
that Robert Barclay in the same section declares that
in "FORMAL" singing "oftentimes great and horrid
lies are said in the sight of God" by "wicked, profane
people," who "take upon them to personate the
experiences and conditions of blessed David," &c.

We have no reason to doubt the truth of what the Apologist says :—" Wicked, profane people" are always acting wickedly ; but we quite fail to understand in this any objection to singing rightly conducted in the true spirit of worship.

As well might we say that Barclay objects to *all* outward manifestations of worship, as being "superstition, will-worship, and abominable idolatry; because in the opening of Prop. xi. he says, "*All other worship* then, both praises, *prayers, or preachings, which man* sets about in his own will, and at his own appointment, which he can both begin and end at his pleasure, do or leave undone as himself seeth meet, whether they be a prescribed form, as a liturgy, &c., or prayers conceived extempore by the natural strength and faculty of the mind, they are all but superstition, will-worship, and abominable idolatry in the sight of God."

"Apology," p. 160.

That Barclay himself never meant to cast any doubt upon the propriety of singing, under the guidance of the spirit, is sufficiently evident : for if he and his fellow-professors had desired to exclude singing altogether from the outward acts of religious worship, is it possible to suppose that he, a prince amongst disputants, "distinguished by strong mental powers," and educated amongst a people accustomed to sing several long hymns at all their assemblies of worship, could have concluded his great argument with the following summing up, from which all idea of so radical a change as the abolition of singing is entirely absent: "So that to conclude, the worship, preaching,

"Apology," Prop. xi. § 28 pp. 190, 191.

praying, and singing, which we PLEAD FOR, is such as
proceedeth from the Spirit of God, and is always
accompanied with its influence, being begun by its
motion, and carried on by the power and strength
thereof : and so is a worship purely spiritual, such as
the Scripture holds forth—John iv. 23, 24 ; 1 Cor.
xiv. 15 : Eph. vi. 18, &c.

"But the worship, preaching, praying, and singing,
which our adversaries plead for, and which we oppose,
is a worship which is both begun, carried on, and
concluded in man's own natural will and strength,
without the motion or influence of God's Spirit, which
they judge they need not wait for : and, therefore,
may be truly performed, both as to the matter and
manner, by the wickedest of men. Such was the
worship and vain oblations which God always rejected,
as appears from Isa. lxvi. 3., Jer. xiv. 12, &c : Isa. i. 13,
Prov. xv. 29, John ix. 31."

To most minds the above summing up would by
itself be conclusive : but before leaving Robert Barclay
we will make one extract from his book, "Truth
cleared of Calumnies." Replying to the writer of a
book entitled "A Dialogue between a Quaker and a
Stable Christian," and in answer to the assertion
"that Singing of Psalms is an Ordinance of Jesus
Christ," he says, "If thou understandest that Singing
of Psalms was used by the Saints, that it is a Part
of God's Worship when performed in His Will and by
His Spirit, and that yet it may be, and is warrantably
performed among the Saints, IT IS A THING DENIED

"Truth cleared
of Calumnies,"
London edition.
1717, p. 55.

BY NO QUAKER (SO CALLED) AND IT IS NOT UNUSUAL
AMONG THEM; whereof I have myself been a witness,
and have felt of the sweetness and quickening Virtue
of the Spirit therein, and at such occasions ministered.
And that at times David's words may also be used, as
the Spirit leads thereunto, and as they suit the condition of the party, is acknowledged without dispute :
but that *without the Spirit, in self-will*, not regarding
how the thing suits their condition, for a mixed mul-
titude to use and sing the expressions of blessed
David, we deny."

Turning now to the "Journal of George Fox," we
find his testimony not less explicit in teaching the
right place of singing, by example, illustration, and
precept.

First, his own *personal example*, not in meeting
exactly, but in Carlisle Jail in 1653 : "I could get up
to the grate, where sometimes I took in my meat, at
which the jailer was often offended. One time he
came in a great rage and beat me with a great cudgel,
though I was not at the grate at that time ; and as he
beat me he cried, "Come out of the window," though
I was then far enough from it. While he struck me I
was made to sing in the Lord's power : and that made
him rage the more. Then he fetched a fiddler, and
brought him in where I .was, and set him to play,
thinking to vex me thereby ; but while he played I
was moved in the everlasting power of the LORD God
to sing ; and MY VOICE DROWNED THE NOISE OF THE
FIDDLE, AND STRUCK AND CONFOUNDED THEM, and made

"Journal of
George Fox,"
Vol. i. p. 160,
7th edition,
London.

them give over fiddling and go their way." No *silent* singing this!

We next take an *illustration* which occurred at Johnstons, in Scotland, in 1657. George Fox writes,

"As they guarded us through the town, James Lancaster *was moved to sing with a melodious sound* in the power of God ; and I was moved to proclaim the day of the Lord, and preach the everlasting gospel to the people." (From which it appears that Sankey and Moody were not the first to engage in this kind of service in Scotland.)

An illustration of congregational singing is given in the account of his visit to the south of Ireland in 1669.

He writes, " Meetings were very large, Friends coming to them far and near ; and other people flocking in. The powerful presence of the Lord was preciously felt with and amongst us, whereby many of the world were reached, convinced, and gathered to the truth ; the Lord's flock was increased, and Friends were greatly refreshed and comforted in feeling the love of God. O, the brokenness that was amongst them in the flowings of life ! So that, in the power and Spirit of the Lord, *many together broke out into singing*, even with audible voices, making melody in their hearts."

Turning now for *precept*, we find George Fox writing

in 1648, " I was to bring them off from all the world's fellowships, and prayings, and singings, which stood in *forms without power ;* that their fellowship might be in the Holy Ghost, and in the Eternal Spirit of God ; that they might pray in the Holy Ghost, and sing in the Spirit, and with the grace that comes by Jesus; making melody in their hearts to the Lord, who hath sent His beloved Son to be their Saviour," &c.

In 1653 he writes to Robert Ariss, "Why should not *them that sings* have liberty of conscience to sing in your meetings? I do look upon thee as a competent judge whether they sing in grace or no."

"Inner Life of the Religious Societies of the Commonwealth," 3rd edition, 1879. p. 462.

In a "General Epistle" written by him in 1662, after describing "The worship of God in the Spirit and in the truth" as "the public worship which Christ set up," and "To pray in the Spirit" as "the public prayer set up among the Christians," &c., he goes on to say—"Singing in the Spirit is public; but they that go from the Spirit of God within, they go into the particular singing, inventing this thing and that thing, and then one will do it, and another will not do it, and so there is no true fellowship, because it is not done in the Spirit; and there is no true fellowship in their worshipping nor in their praying, because it is not done in the Spirit; for the true fellowship in singing, in praying, in worshipping of God, is in the Spirit of God."

"Epistles of George Fox," 2nd edition, London, p. 84.

Again he writes in a letter dated 1658—"Now Friends, who have denied the world's songs and singings, sing ye in the Spirit and with grace, making melody in your hearts to the Lord. And ye, having denied the world's formal praying, pray ye always in the Spirit, and watch in it."

"Epistles of George Fox," p. 65.

Eph. vi. 18.

A very misleading mistake has been made by many in supposing that by the words "*in the spirit*" the early Friends and the apostles meant, *in silence.* A very slight examination of the few passages we have already quoted shows how entirely incorrect is this idea. The very last sentence, for example, would in that sense forbid ALL VOCAL and therefore all public PRAYER, for it says, " Pray ye *always* in the Spirit." The words appear to have conveyed to the minds of those who wrote them what we might have expressed by the words, "in heartfelt sincerity and under the guidance and assistance of the Holy Spirit."

Many more confirmatory extracts might be made from the writings of Early Friends, but we will now conclude this portion of our paper with an extract from "The Inner Life of the Religious Societies of the Commonwealth," by the late Robert Barclay, a book of deep and accurate research and sound and unbiassed judgment, which has already taken a first place in the religious historical literature of our day.

The author writes at the commencement of the 19th chapter—"We here break off from the thread of the history, to remark that singing, as well as prayer and preaching, appears to have been acknowledged by George Fox and his coadjutors to be a part of Divine worship, from the commencement of their religious movement, while the carrying out of this practice in public worship was opposed by the Storey and Wilkinson party.

"Inner Life of the Religious Societies of the Commonwealth,' p. 451.

"See also 'Truth's Defence,' p. 21, 1658, by Geo. Fox and R. Hubberthorne ; 'Y. M. Epistle,

1675; * 'Letter of George Fox to Robert Ariss, 1653;' 'Croeses' History,' p. 55, 1696."

## III.—MODERN OBJECTIONS.

We have now seen that the Society of Friends has accorded to Singing a place which is not antagonistic to, but entirely coincident with, Scripture; and, notwithstanding the objections which have been made against the practice by *individuals*, such as Storey, Wilkinson, and others, even to the present time, the Society, as a Society, has kept true to its ancient testimony and never denied that Singing, when entered upon, not formally, but in obedience to, and dependence upon, Divine intimation and guidance, is a very proper, joyful, and comforting portion of Divine Worship.

There are, however, some who acknowledge the truth of what has been written, and agree with our deductions so far as regards the practice and profession of Early Friends, who even say that our argument is indisputable in theory but who stumble at carrying it

---

' This Epistle declares in the Name of the Society, "It hath been, and is, our living sense and constant testimony, according to our experience of the divers operations of the Spirit and Power of God in His Church, that there has been, and is, serious sighing, sensible groaning, and reverent singing, breathing forth a heavenly sound with joy and grace, with the Spirit and with the understanding, which is not to be quenched or discouraged, except immoderate."

From 1675 to 1782 the foregoing extract was circulated in manuscript in every quarterly and monthly meeting in England, in the parchment book which formed the basis of our present "Book of Christian Doctrine, Practice, and Discipline," and it was probably in reference to it that George Gray, "a minister in good estimation," wrote from the Tolbooth of Aberdeen to Friends of Colliehill, in 1676, "Let none speak, nor sing, nor sigh, nor groan, but in a true sense of their conditions." See "Diary of Alexander Jaffray," p. 437, London, 1833.

out into practice, urging many objections. We will,
therefore, proceed to examine some of these objections,
confining ourselves to those which we have actually
heard stated.

*Obj.* 1.—The Society has not practised Singing for
the last 100 years, which is in itself an argument
against its reintroduction.

*Ans.*—This objection infers that the long-continued
avoidance of an act of worship is a reason for its con-
tinued suppression.

We can hardly call such a statement *an argument :*
it is a *doctrine;* and, certainly, not one to be found
in the Bible ; and, therefore, we are not bound to
believe it. It is a dangerous doctrine, leading to
the enquiry as to how long it is necessary to cease
from an act of worship before its absence justifies
its omission ? Could the false seducers, of whom
it is written in 2 Peter ii. 15, "Which have
forsaken the right way, and are gone astray," have
pleaded it in excuse ! Would a backslider of fifty
years' standing come within its scope, or does it need
a whole century to elapse before becoming valid ?
But if it *be* an argument, then powerful indeed must
the argument have been against the introduction of
silent worship in the 17th century ! for had not such
worship been omitted for generations ? And whether
it be doctrine or argument, it is alike opposed to the
advice of George Fox, who wrote, "Keep your testimony for your liberty in Christ Jesus, and stand fast

in it, against all the false liberties in old Adam ; and your liberty in the Spirit of God, and in the Gospel of Christ Jesus, against all the false and loose liberties in the flesh."

"And this worship He set up, and preached up above sixteen hundred years since : many hundred years before Mass Book, Common Prayer Book, Directory, or Church Faith were. And this was the public worship that Christ set up in the Spirit and in the Truth."

*Obj.* 2.—Although it is evident that Singing was practised amongst early Friends, yet, after a century of nonuse of the practice, it should not now be allowed in any meeting without special recognition from the Yearly Meeting.

*Ans.*—Suppressing for the present the Scriptural reply, we will here simply state that it is generally thought that the time occupied in the necessary business of the Yearly Meeting is quite sufficient without adding to it the periodical reaffirmation of every detail of religious belief and practice. The *principle* for which we contend has been reaffirmed over and over again. We will quote but one, so late as in the Epistle of 1860.

"The true worshipper is he who is resigned to every intimation of the Divine will; not prejudging the counsels of his Lord, nor allowing any habits or fears of his own to bring him under a bondage wherein the word of the Lord can neither have free course nor be glorified."

*Side notes:*
"Epistles of George Fox," p. 102. 1667

"Book of Doctrine, Practice, and Discipline," c. ii. § 1, p. 34.

*Obj. 3.*—But we are evidently not prepared for the introduction of singing into *our* particular meeting; and, therefore, we conscientiously oppose its introduction elsewhere, and think others should be subject in this matter.

*Ans.*—We reply with a quotation from William Penn. Speaking of the Society of Friends, he says, Preface to "George Fox's Journal." p. 26. "They distinguish between imposing any practice that immediately regards faith or worship (which is never to be done, nor suffered, or submitted unto), and requiring Christian compliance with those methods that only respect Church-business, in its more civil part and concern, and that regard the discreet and orderly maintenance of the character of the Society, as a sober and religious community."

From which it will be seen that to forbid the carrying out of this practice when engaged in with the unanimous consent and approval of the members in any particular meeting  it being a "practice that immediately regards" "worship," is not opposed to Scripture, nor to the published documents of the Society, nor affecting "the discreet and orderly maintenance of the character of the Society as a sober and religious community,"—is a violation of that compact which holds us together as a Christian body, and "is never to be done, nor suffered or submitted unto." It is indeed a giving way to that spirit of evil which, in the past history of the Church of Christ, has borne such sad and bitter fruit of separation and disunion, Matt vii. 12. and is a breach of the golden rule, "Therefore all things whatsoever ye would that men should do to you, do ye even so to them."

*Obj.* 4. But if we were to recognize congregations where such a practice is upheld it would be impossible to confine it within the limits of such congregations, and members from those meetings would attempt to introduce the practice where it was not approved.

*Ans.* This, we submit, is a faithless fear. Those who, in the early days of our Society, sought wisdom from God in arranging for the orderly carrying out of their religious views, did not forget that they were legislating for men and women whose gifts, however brilliant, were still in "earthen vessels," and therefore rightly made provision for the appointment of "*Elders*," who, in sympathy with the meeting, should watch over the ministry for good, carefully guarding against anything that should cause unpleasantness or want of harmony in the solemn act of congregational worship. And in the exercise of so weighty a responsibility, the Elders are not left without instruction in the Book of books; for there is firstly, the commandment, "That he who loveth God, love his brother also," and secondly, the test of sincerity. "By this shall all men know that ye are my disciples, if ye have love one to another." Those who are true to this command and answer to this test are not the ones, wherever their lot may be cast, wittingly to cause any unpleasantness or breach of love by introducing a practice which is not approved; and all others who enter into religious service whilst

1 John iv. 21.

John xiii. 35.

out of this spirit of love to God and love to man, are
not only out of harmony with true Friends everywhere,
but, if professing to act under Divine guidance, are
Matt. vii. 15. most aptly described in Bible language as "wolves" in
"sheep's clothing." Where therefore in any meeting
there is, from any cause, a want of Christian unity in
this exercise, and where, in the words which we have
Page 23. already quoted from George Fox, "one will do it, and
another will not do it, and so there is no true fellowship," the very essence of spiritual communion is
lacking. And where the exercise of this gift is found to
Gal. v. 20, 26; produce "variance, emulations, wrath, strife," so that
vi. 2. the children of a loving Father are "provoking one
another," not willing to "bear one another's burdens
and so fulfil the law of Christ," in such a meeting,
we emphatically say, singing is *not* expedient ; let the
Eph. iv. 15. Elders there stand to their posts, "speaking the truth
in love,"—for God is not the author of confusion, and
His good Spirit will not require any to light the fires
of discord with His precious gifts of grace.

Just as earthly parents rejoice when the pre-
sents they have bestowed upon their children give
pleasure to their dear ones, but all their joy is turned
to sorrow when the little ones disagree over them, so
Ps. cxlix. 4. our Heavenly Father "taketh pleasure in His people"
as they rejoice together in the exercise of His gifts,
John xvii. 22, 23. praising Him in the answered prayer, "That they may
be one, even as we are one : I in them, and thou in
me, that they may be made perfect in one."

*Obj.* 5.—If the practice were recognized in some meetings and disapproved in others it could not be satisfactorily placed under the ordinary "Eldership."

*Ans.*—This, we believe, is an imaginary difficulty. Mark the gift of the Elder. It is a gift which can only be rightly exercised in harmony with the meeting. So essential is this that ample security for it is provided in our rules, by the mode of election to that office, by the regular and frequent revision of the list of Elders, and by the provision made that in changing the residence from one Quarterly Meeting to another the office becomes thereby vacated.

The Elder who is in perfect sympathy with those who are enjoying the "strong meat," may be unable to comprehend the feelings of those who are being delighted with the first-tasted sweets of "the sincere milk of the word." *Heb. v. 12, 14.* *1 Pet. ii. 2.*

The true Elder, therefore, "resigned to every intimation of the Divine will, not prejudging the counsels of his Lord, nor allowing any habits or fears of his own to bring him under a bondage," will seek to be baptized into sympathy with the rightly exercised and tender spirits with whom he has assembled ; and as he is faithful, he will be endued with the spirit of " love and of a sound mind," and enabled to act with judgment and wise discrimination. *Page 27.* *2 Tim. i. 7.*

*Obj.* 6.—If we were to admit singing as a recognized act of worship in any of our meetings it would prove only the thin end of the wedge : soon we should want

a choir and vocal music, which could not be provided
without the introduction of an instrument, and even
then would be impossible without a pre-arrangement of
hymns, and so it would inevitably lead to exhibitions
of the whole paraphernalia of formality and deadness,
too common around us already.

*Ans.* It would be amusing, were it not sad, to see
with what old worn-out weapons the truth continues
to be assailed.

Many will recall the evil prophecies that were heard
on the first establishment of First-day Schools, Reading
Meetings, Prayer Meetings, Christian Missions, &c.,
each one of which was "only the thin end of the
wedge" that would break in sunder our only protection
from formalism, decay, and death. If any will use
such arguments, let them at least be consistent and
forbid preaching, lest it should lead to a stole and a
gown, to advowsons and cathedrals; and prayer also,
lest it should lead to genuflexions, postures, and pros-
trations!

The fact is, that the more boldly we act up to and
act out our true principles, the more clearly defined
will they become, and by contrast the more distinctly
will be shown out those things against which we *have*
a testimony to bear.

*Obj.* 7.—Though the last objection may be too
sweeping, yet if Singing be allowed there is great
danger of the introduction of vocal and instrumental
music.

*Ans.*- We have lost sight of our principles and substituted prejudices, and as a necessary consequence danger on this head has already arisen in some meetings, and it is only by holding our true testimony intelligently that this real danger will be avoided.

With perfect consistency the Society of Friends has discouraged the use of instrumental music in worship, for the following reasons amongst others.

1. No command or precept is found under the Christian dispensation for its use.

2. There is no command to glorify God in instruments of our own manufacture; but we read, "Glorify God in your body and in your spirit, which are God's."  *1 Cor. vi. 20.*

3. Music, so far as it consists of sounds proceeding from dead instruments, can hardly with any truth be called the outward manifestation of inward spiritual worship, as, we think, all acts of worship *should be.*

4. Whilst few will deny that the love of music is inherent in our human nature, and, if kept in subordination to the high purposes of our existence, may be refining and ennobling, so that we may enjoy music as we enjoy other innocent recreations, yet our outward enjoyment is not worship. And although the emotion produced by instrumental music may, and, we hopefully trust, often does, lead to true worship (as may also a beautiful landscape, a touching picture, or an exquisite piece of statuary), yet there is reason to fear that the emotion is often mistaken for worship, and consequently proves a very dangerous and false rest.

5. Whilst the human voice, with all its wonderful power of varied modulation and expression, is a Divine gift, free to all who sing, manufactured instruments of music require to be purchased, and it is out of the question to suppose that God can be worshipped more satisfactorily by those who are sufficiently wealthy to purchase an instrument than by those who are poor and needy.

6. Most of these objections equally extend to that high-class singing very properly distinguished by the Early Friends as *vocal music*, or "artificial music by voice," which is generally costly, can only be learned by a course of training under an able master, and necessitates singing by a choir and prearrangement of the hymns to be sung. Against this we undoubtedly have a testimony to bear; but the singing of which *we approve* requires no further outward learning than is necessary in learning to speak.

7. There is a fundamental difference between—First, religious emotions which owe their origin to influences outside of ourselves, as those produced by looking upon Nature's wonders, contemplating works of art, or listening to sweet harmonies; and, Secondly, those religious emotions produced by the Holy Spirit itself upon our hearts, which, having their origin within, manifest themselves outwards in preaching, prayer, or singing.

To avoid a lengthy dissertation, we will endeavour to show this difference by putting a few questions.

What congregation under the influence of religious

feeling would, individually or collectively, hasten to gaze upon a landscape, however lovely?

Where would we find the company that, either in public or private, would yearn to give expression to godly joy or sorrow by an exercise in painting or statuary?

How many earnest Christians are there in the churches who long to show their joy by calling upon the organist for a solo, or the choir to sing the pure music by "lah-ing" the notes?

But on the other hand, where is the loving Christian that has learned to sing who has not again and again found the emotions of his heart bubbling over in the words and tune of some beautiful melody? and how often is it found in churches where Christian liberty is given for this exercise that a sweet communion of spirit is felt both in the desire for, and the choice of, the hymn?

For these and other reasons, whilst approving of singing, Friends have consistently condemned instrumental and "vocal music," or "artificial music by voice," as parts of public worship, as will be seen by the following quotations :—

"But as to their artificial music, either by organs or other instruments or *voice*, we have neither example nor precept for it in the New Testament." "Barclay's Apology," § xxvi. ¶ 11.

"That which is of the character ordinarily designated as sacred music not unfrequently stimulates expressions and feelings which are far from being the genuine breathings of a renewed heart, and tends to produce Printed Epistle, 1854. "Doctrine, Practice, and Discipline," p. 120.

an excitement often unhappily mistaken for devotion, and to withdraw the soul from that quiet, humble, and retired frame, in which prayer and praise may be truly offered with the spirit and with the understanding also."

"Apology for the True Christian Divinity, Vindicated from John Brown's Examination and pretended Confutation." By Robert Barclay, 1679. § xii. ¶ 6.

"And whereas he asketh *Whether the Spirit inspireth the metre in the song, and the tone of the Singing?* He showeth his folly and lightness, while he ridiculously supposeth that metre is necessary, or any other tone, than nature has given to everyone; of which God by His Spirit maketh use as an instrument, as he doth of other parts and faculties of the body to the performing of spiritual duties." *

*Obj.* 8.—If singing is allowed at all, it should only be what is commonly called Solo singing; that is, by *one* singing to the rest, and not congregational singing.

Neh. viii. 6.
Ps. cxli. 2.
1 Tim. ii. 8.

Ex. ix. 29.
Ezra ix. 5.

Matt. vi. 5.
Luke xviii. 13.

2 Chr. vi. 13.
Ps. xcv. 6.

*Ans.*—Throughout the diversity of the teaching of the Bible there runs a chord of perfect harmony. In the act of prayer we read of *lifting up* the hands, of *spreading abroad* the hands, of *standing*, of *kneeling*. So in singing we find much variety of mode, as if even in this indirect manner the lesson was intended to be taught that the Lord looks upon the heart and does not rejoice in any outward form of manifestation more than another, but rather, in condescension to our

---

* The question as to the use of an instrument by a travelling missionary to whom is entrusted the Gift of Song, as in the case of Ira D. Sankey, is not entered upon here, as being too wide for our present paper and involving important considerations quite apart from the regular, ordinary use of an instrument in public worship.

Nor do we touch upon the question of music in the home.

human weakness, which delights in variety, he would satisfy us in this also as we keep close to our Guide, who alone can safely lead us, avoiding alike the Scylla of Formalism on the one hand and the Charybdis of Fashion on the other. Thus we find *Solos* in Deut. xxxi. 30, and 2 Sam. xxii. 1; *Duets* in Judg. v. 1, and Acts xvi. 25; and *Hymns, joined in by whole companies,* in Ex. xv. 1, Neh. xii. 42, and Matt. xxvi. 30.

*Obj.* 9.—But if a whole congregation join in singing a hymn, those who cannot truly unite in the expressions used are guilty of hypocrisy.

*Ans.*—This is a specious error, and has no true warrant either in the Bible or in the approved writings of Friends.

If men move to perform outward acts of worship, or to lead others to do so, *in their own strength and power and will, and without heart service,* they are but simulating acts and expressions of devotion which are not felt, and therefore the whole exercise is hypocrisy, as the Early Friends declared over and over again. But mark, they never charged individuals of such congregations with hypocrisy. *That* judgment they left with the Omniscient, where we also shall be wise to leave it.

But the case is entirely altered where, *waiting for the Spirit's power and direction,* the servants of the Lord are moved in the constraining love of Christ to lead to outward acts of preaching, prayer, or praise.

In such congregations there need be no hypocrisy—not even in those who are out of communion in spirit, unless, *with a purpose, knowingly and wilfully to* DECEIVE, *they personate feelings and experiences not their own.* But if, without intent to deceive, the actions or words of any are unaccompanied with the love of God in their hearts, we have Scripture warrant for saying that though they "speak with the tongues of men and of angels," they are "become as sounding brass or a tinkling cymbal." No change of posture, no words, no sounds, can in any degree alter that sad and terrible state. Call them spiritually dead if you like—they were so when they walked into the meeting, when they took their seats, when they sat in solemn silence—but call them not hypocrites, for that implies those who feign to be what they are not, and who pretend to virtues which they have not ; who, like the Pharisees of old, approve of the Good, whilst yet they deliberately shut the door of their hearts against the Spirit and choose the Evil, though still *pretending to be good.*

1 Cor. xiii. 1.

*Obj.* 10.—But tender souls and loving, trusting Christians will sometimes find that they cannot perfectly unite in all the sentiments of a hymn in which they are asked to join.

*Ans.*—Certainly ! and so also they will sometimes find a similar difficulty in joining in public prayer and in uniting with the sentiments of a preacher.

In such cases they hold themselves at liberty *not* to

unite, and no exercise allows this liberty to be availed of so easily and so decidedly as singing.

*Obj.* 11.—But sometimes a stranger has proposed a hymn which the congregation could **not sing**, not knowing the tune.

*Ans.*—Even the apostles were gradually, and not without some failures, led from the bondage of the ceremonial law into the liberty of Christ. Let us not take their failures as arguments against Christianity, nor our failures as arguments against Christian liberty; but rather pray more faithfully for clearness of spiritual perception. *(Acts x. 15; xi. 2, 3; xxiv. 21. Gal. ii. 11.)*

But if, under a *right* sense of Divine requirement, a hymn has been chosen which cannot be sung by the meeting, the burden of duty may be relieved either (as the *Spirit* may intimate) by the proposer singing it *alone*, or by *reading* the hymn, or by choosing another of similar import, or by sitting down and leaving the hymn unsung. We have known the last-named action to produce a marked effect in turning the thoughts of many upon the subject matter of the hymn after the meeting had separated. And such action has its parallel in the case of ministers who have sometimes stood up to preach but have had to resume their seats before proceeding, and wait for clearer light or for the gift of more spiritual power.

*Obj.* 12.—We have heard an objection to the use of a hymn book, asking if the choice of it was inspired.

See p. 36.

*Ans.*—We fear this objection is suspiciously like that which John Brown made when he derisively asked Robert Barclay if the metre and tone were inspired.

All that is necessary to make a hymn book acceptable is, that it contain hymns which express the sentiments and feelings appertaining to true spiritual worship, which all good hymn books will be found to do ; and which is no more extraordinary than that many languages should each be able to serve the religious wants of mankind.

*Obj.* 13.—We are equally convinced with you that if the Lord calls for Singing it must be right, and make no reservation in this ; but we assert that the Lord does not require it ; you mistake His call, and are claiming higher authority than you have any right to claim.

*Ans.*—We are humbly grateful for all reminders of our need for constant watchfulness in seeking to know our Master's will concerning the exercise of His spiritual gifts. But that Master gives us much encouragement ; and either His promises are true, or they are not. If they *are* true we ought to believe such as the following, and in believing them there is neither pride nor presumption, but child-like trust.

Ps. xxxii. 8

"I will instruct thee and teach thee in the way which thou shalt go : I will guide thee with mine eye."

John xiv. 26.

" But the Comforter, which is the Holy Ghost, whom

the Father will send in my name, he shall teach you all things."

"If any of you lack wisdom, let him ask of God, that giveth to all men liberally and upbraideth not; and it shall be given him." Jas. i. 5.

"But ye have an unction from the Holy One, and ye know all things." 1 John ii. 20.

*Obj.* 14.—"No doubt but ye are the people, and wisdom shall die with you. But I have understanding as well as you; I am not inferior to you: yea, who knoweth not such things as these?" Job xii. 2.

*Ans.*—Very far be it from us to claim any superiority of wisdom or knowledge, but we would lovingly urge that in the practical carrying out of religious service, as in all other things not definitely revealed in the Scriptures of Truth, whilst there is abundant promise of heavenly guidance and wisdom (coupled with the intimation that to his own Master each shall stand or fall), there is not a word to encourage any to expect an answer to the query, "Lord, and what shall this man do?" further than that already given, "What is that to thee? follow thou me;" but there is enough to John xxi. 21, 22. show that the will of the Lord is, that in non-essentials Christian brethren must "judge not, that" they "be not judged," but earnestly and faithfully commend Matt. vii. 1. one another in prayer "unto him that is able to keep" them "from falling, and to present" them "faultless Jude 24. before the presence of his glory with exceeding joy."

## IV.—UNANSWERABLE OBJECTIONS.

It now only remains to quote three unanswerable arguments, each the type of many of a similar character.

*Obj.* 1.—"I hope I may not live to see the day when Singing is allowed in any Friends' meeting."

Would it not have sounded more like the voice of a disciple, to have said, "If it be the will of the Lord that a meeting where Singing is allowed should be recognized, may He open my understanding to perceive it and help me to speed the recognition?"

*Obj.* 2.—"If anyone were to give out a hymn at" [my meeting] "I would put on my hat and walk out."

Would it not have been more consistent with the character of a Christian adviser, to have said, "Whatever others were to do, my duty would be to stand true to my trust, and, not prejudging the will of my Lord, seek to be divinely guided and faithfully to act as a watchman set upon Zion's wall?"

*Obj.* 3.—"If singing were to be introduced into" [my meeting] "I would leave the Society."

Would it not have been more in accord with the usual affability and courtesy of the true Christian, to have said, "I will very seriously and prayerfully consider its effect as a help or a hindrance in my Christian course, and then, if necessary to review the grounds of my connection with the Society, I will do so under a sense of my responsibility to the church and to my Heavenly Father, in nothing acting hastily, but only step by step as the Great Head of the Church shall lead the way."

The above remarks are not made in any captious or censorious spirit, but on the contrary, under a sympathetic and keenly appreciative sense of the feeling which gave birth to the expressions, induced by the vivid realization of the unhappiness and discomfort produced by a sudden and radical change in personal religious habits when caused by others, and not resulting from a change of one's own convictions.

But why should any permit themselves to stand aghast at a mere creation of the imagination? No sudden change, no dire alteration of habits, customs, or manners in any meeting is asked for or expected, by those who advocate Christian liberty to sing. Such a revolution appears to be demanded only by those who refuse to acknowledge meetings held according to the principles of Friends, unless they accept such a change and give up the liberty of singing; whilst even many of those who hold out this condition believe the members of such meetings would not be wise to accept it, for they say "We think singing quite right and very suitable in a Mission meeting like yours;" but change the word "*Mission*" to "Friends" and the case becomes altered in their estimation, and the practice quite wrong! as if what was right under one name could be wrong under another!

But nevertheless such objections as those which we have last quoted—made use of, no doubt, under feelings of grief and pain, not perhaps to be wondered at— may be overruled for good, by being made useful warnings to others not to be cast down and discouraged by differences of opinion even from those upon whose judgment they would gladly lean. Bearing in themselves the signs of human weakness, incompatible with that teachable and obedient spirit into which it should be our prayer to be baptized, sentiments of this character remind us that only as we look unto Jesus and away from all earthly dependence shall we reap the fulness of the promise already quoted —" I will instruct thee and teach thee in the way which thou shalt go: I will guide thee with mine eye."

Ps. xxxii. 8.

## IS SINGING EXPEDIENT ?

"Ye are the light of the world.  A city that is set Matt. v. 14 on an hill cannot be hid."  "Let your light so shine Matt. v. 16 before men, that they may see your good works and glorify your Father which is in heaven."

Many of our own Members do not appear to see the fundamental principle upon which our testimony on the question before us, as upon all worship, is based.

One, for example, declared that if we only knew by experience, as he had known, the bitter bondage of formal singing, from which in the meetings of Friends he had found a glad deliverance, we should very thankfully rejoice in the absence of all singing.

No language can over-paint the dread and horror which we have of the degrading bondage of forced religious exercises.  We rejoice with any who have come out of that bondage.  But why only change into another, mild indeed though it be compared with the former, the bondage of total silence and abstention ? Let us rather hasten forward into the promised land of perfect liberty, the special heritage of the children of God, in which liberty we may rejoicingly say :—

"I want to praise, with life renewed,
    As I never praised before ;
With voice and pen, with song and speech,
    To praise Thee more and more,
And the gladness and the gratitude
    Rejoicingly outpour.

From "Loyal Responses," by Frances Ridley Havergal, p. 86.

" I long to praise Thee more, and yet
  This is no care to me :
If Thou shalt fill my mouth with songs,
  Then I will sing to Thee ;
And if my silence praise Thee best,
  Then silent I will be."

But if, as we have seen above, our own members do not all fully comprehend the true principle of Gospel liberty in religious worship, very many in other denominations are still further from its right apprehension, as may be gathered from the following queries, selected from a number contained in a circular addressed by an evangelical vicar to his parishioners :—

"4. Do you like, or object to, the use of Anthems?

"5. Do you prefer the present system of 'Services,' or plain chants for the Canticles?

"6. Do you like the responses in the Services chanted, or monotoned, or simply made by the Congregation?

"7. Do you consider that the present system of music is a help or a hindrance to you in heartfelt worship?"

The 7th question will show that the circular is the production of one who realizes that "*heartfelt worship*" is what the church of God requires, outward arrangements being only helps or hindrances thereto.

But the 4th, 5th, and 6th questions will show better than any words of ours could do, some of the musical difficulties which, under their present system, even the best-intentioned ministers have to meet.

And how, for them, does the light of those who

indiscriminately oppose all Singing, shine upon these questions?

Is it not all darkness? For the advice, "Cease all Singing," inconsistent as it is with human instincts, and unsupported by Scripture, is felt to be as unsatisfying as was the direction to George Fox, to take tobacco, when, in trouble of mind, he sought for direction and help.

Therefore, surely it *is* expedient, for the enlightenment of the world and the upholding of our ancient testimonies, that our light should shine clearly, and that every fold of the old banner given us to bear should be "displayed because of the truth."     Ps. lx. 4.

Let us once more, in drawing to a close, rehearse the two points in the fundamental principle of worship which we have been considering.

1. All true and acceptable worship to God is offered in the inward and immediate moving and drawing of His own Spirit, and in implicit obedience thereto. There must be no withholding, no reservation, if the full blessing is to be enjoyed : all, both men and women, are to follow the Divine guidance into whatsoever line of service .it may lead. There must be no unspoken refrain *unconsciously* breathed—a reservation which, if expressed in words, would be utterly repudiated :—"Whatsoever He saith unto you, do it,"   John ii. 5. *unless He bids you* SING!" "To obey is better than   1 Sam. xv. 22. sacrifice, and to hearken than the fat of rams," *except in the matter of* SINGING! "We ought to obey God   Acts v. 29

rather than men," *unless* it be an intimation to sing !
Rather let us pray for *implicit* obedience, and cry,

Ps. xliii. 3.
"O send out Thy light and Thy truth : let them lead
me."

2. This worship will, and necessarily must, be
heart-worship.    True Singing is that alone which
proceeds from the heart.    It need not manifest itself
by sounds which are melodious in the ears of others.
The sea-gull may as truly praise God by its wild
scream as the nightingale with its mellifluous song—

Psalm cxlviii.
8, 9.
"the stormy wind fulfilling His word," as effectually
as the silent "mountains and all hills"—the untutored
voice of an old illiterate woman, as the unspoken
adoration of the educated lady.

"Diary of
Mrs. Kitty
Trevyiyan."
p. 253.
"When I sat by mother in the quiet afternoon, I
told her something of what father had said : and she
told me how it had gladdened her as she lay there, to
hear Betty singing hymns in her dear old cracked
voice as she went about her work.

"'I am afraid, Kitty,' she said, 'I have been too
dainty about words and forms.    The holy angels, no
doubt, do not need the delicate spices of quaint
fancies to make the true prayers and praises of the
poorest sweet as incense to them.    I felt it to-day, as
I lay here, and found the smell of the dewy grass and
the new-mown hay sweeter than any perfume, and the
sound of Betty's Wesleyan hymns sweet as the singing
of a cathedral choir.    Yet still,' she added smiling,
'my own thoughts flowed back into the channel of
old Herbert's poetry, and I sang in my heart—

" ' My joy, my life, my crown !
 My heart was meaning all the day,
 Somewhat it fain would say ;
And still it runneth, muttering up and down,
With only this, ' My joy, my life, my crown !' ' "

WE need—THE WORLD needs—the great principle as
to the character of true worship, true praise, to be so
ingrained into our habits of thought, that no droning
in perfect discord, however harsh to ears trained to
tune and time, shall be able to mar the effect of that
which, by the communion of the Spirit, we know to
be genuine praise.*

And therefore it *is* expedient that we continue
steadfastly to uphold this principle.

## CONCLUSION.

" Whilst it is at all times the duty of members of
the church faithfully to maintain the truth, and whilst
some of them may rightly feel themselves called upon
openly to oppose error, we believe that there is hardly
anything more inimical to the growth of vital religion
than indulgence in the spirit of religious controversy.
\* \* \*  If he, our soul's enemy, can but introduce

Printed Epistle,
1846.
"Doctrine,
Practice, and
Discipline,"
ch. ii. § 7, p. 72.

---

' Musicians may feel discord to be " torture," and deem it impossible to
overcome this natural sensitiveness. But in our state by nature is it not
equally impossible to control our feelings in order to obey the command—
"Love your enemies?" Matt. v. 44. In both cases, as in all others where
the path of duty lies, the Christian may find the truth of the text, " I can do
all things through Christ which strengtheneth me." Phil. iv. 13.

D

men into his spirit, he cares little how true may be their words."

May we all be preserved from this controversial spirit! Humbly and lovingly is this paper sent forth to my fellow-members, under a solemn and weighty sense of religious duty, and with the earnest desire and prayer that the true Christian liberty for which our Society from the first has contended, and which is always consistent with the "unity of the Spirit in the bond of peace," may, under the Divine blessing, be thereby proclaimed and upheld; and that in, and through, and above all, the will of the Lord may be done.

Eph. iv. 3.